Body Works

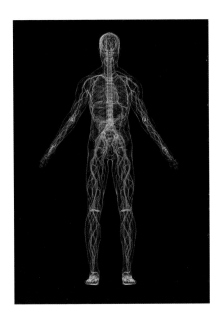

Written by Bridie Dickson

Flying Start
to Literacy®

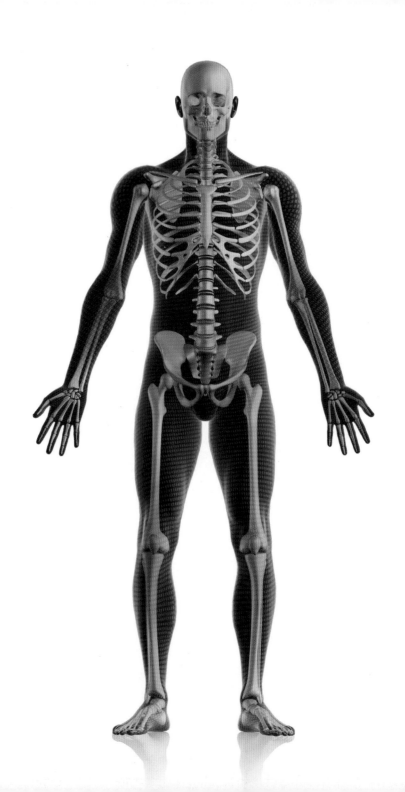

Contents

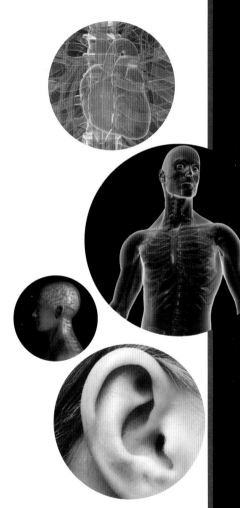

Introduction

Your body has many different parts.
These parts work together to keep you
alive. They enable your body to do things
such as breathe, move, think, feel, see
and hear.

This book will help you to learn about how
your body works.

Your heart

Your body has a heart that is beating all the time. Each time your heart beats it pumps blood around your body. When you are resting, your heart beats between 60 and 100 times per minute.

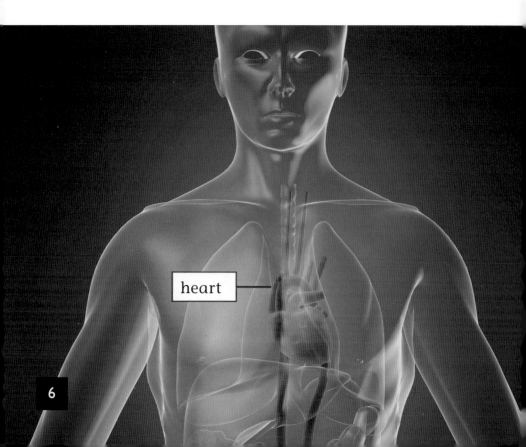

heart

Try this ...

Put two fingers on your neck, just under your jaw. Press gently to find your pulse.

Count how many times you feel your pulse beat in one minute.

Now run for one minute. Count your pulse again. What do you notice? Why do you think it has changed?

Your lungs

Your body needs oxygen to stay alive. Your body gets oxygen by breathing in air. The air goes in through your nose and mouth and into your lungs. The lungs put oxygen into your blood and your heart pumps it around your body.

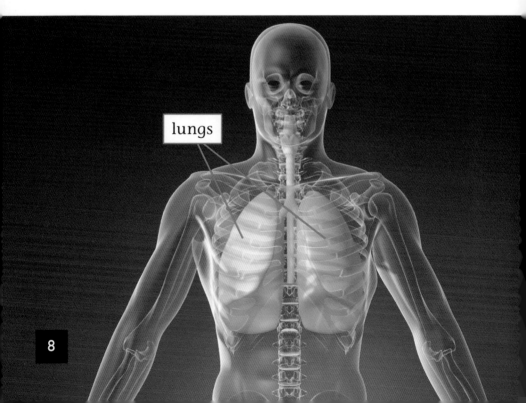

lungs

Try this ...

Count how many times you breathe in and out in one minute.

Now run for one minute.

Count how many times you breathe in and out in one minute now.

What do you notice? What do you think has changed and why?

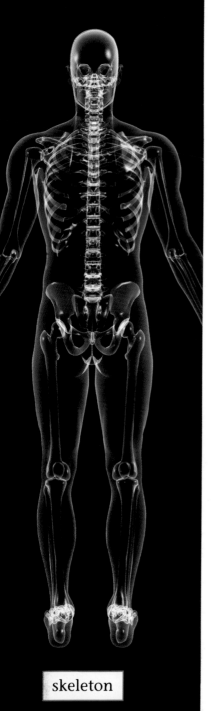

skeleton

Your skeleton

Your body has bones that fit together to make a frame called a skeleton.

Your skeleton gives your body its shape and it also protects your heart, lungs, brain and other internal organs.

arm span

Try this ...

Stand up straight. Use a piece of string to measure your height. Use another piece of string to measure your arm span. Put the two pieces of string together.

What do you notice? Is your height and arm span the same length or is it different?

Your muscles

Your body has muscles. Most muscles are attached to bones and help your body to move. These muscles move your bones when you do things like running or jumping or swimming.

Other muscles, such as your heart and the muscles that help you breathe, work all the time to keep you alive.

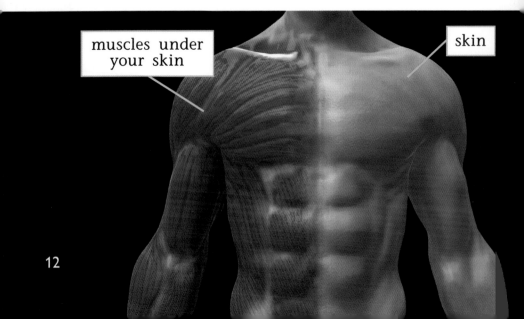

muscles under
your skin

skin

12

Try this ...

Hold your friend's arm. Ask your friend to close his or her hand tightly and then to open it again.

What can you feel? Can you feel the muscles working?

Your brain

Your brain controls your body and makes your muscles move. When you are running, your brain makes your heart beat faster so more blood is pumped around your body.

Your brain allows you to store information so that you can learn, solve problems and remember. Your brain also controls your feelings.

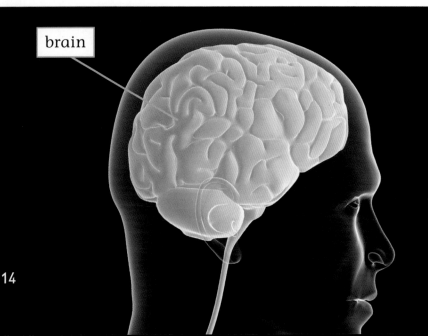

brain

Try this ...

Place five objects on a table.
Ask a friend to look at the objects.

After five seconds cover the objects.
Can your friend name the objects?

Now you do it. How many objects
can you remember?

Your skin

Your body is covered with skin. Your skin stops germs and dirt from getting into your body.

Your skin can feel if something is too hot or too cold. Your skin stretches so that your body can move.

The skin on your body is being replaced all the time. As skin cells die, new ones are made to replace them.

skin

This is what
your skin looks
like close up.

hair

flakes
of skin

Try this ...

Stand in the sunlight.
Rub the back of your hand or leg.

What do you notice?

Some of the tiny specks floating
in the light are your dead skin cells.

Your eyes

Your eyes allow you to see. Light enters your eye through the pupil and goes to the back of your eye and a message is sent to your brain. Your brain then works out what you are looking at.

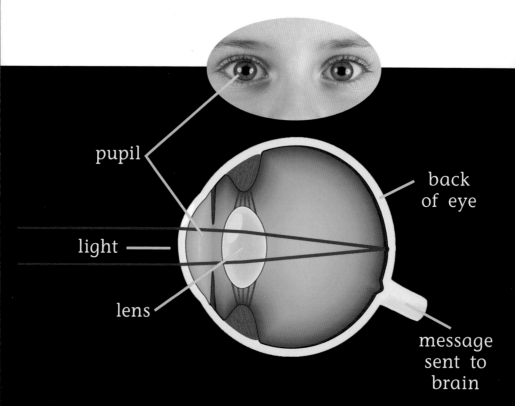

pupil

light —

lens

back of eye

message sent to brain

Try this ...

Look at your
pupils in a mirror.
Close your eyes
and count to 20.
Take your hands
away and look at your pupils.
What do you notice?

Your pupils control how much light
goes into your eyes. In bright light
your pupils become smaller to let in
less light. When it is dark your pupils
become bigger to let in as much
light as possible.

Your ears

Your ears allow you to hear sound.
Sounds enter your ears and a
message is sent to your brain.
Your brain then works out
what sound you are hearing
and where it came from.

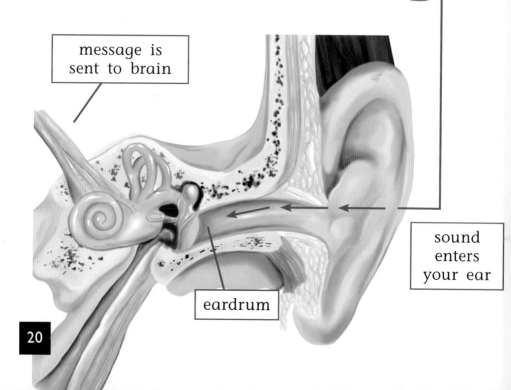

message is
sent to brain

sound
enters
your ear

eardrum

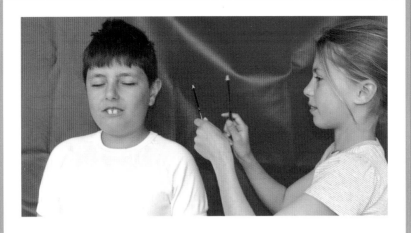

Try this ...

Ask a friend to close his or her eyes.

Hit two pencils together in front of your friend. Then do it to the side of your friend and behind your friend. Ask your friend to point to where the sounds are coming from.

Can your friend tell where the sounds are coming from?

Conclusion

Your body is growing and changing all the time. It does this without you thinking about it. You can help to look after your body by eating healthy food and getting lots of exercise.

Parts of your body

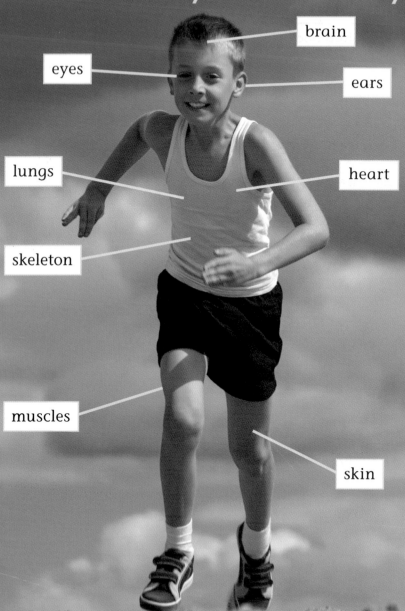

brain

eyes

ears

lungs

heart

skeleton

muscles

skin